The Pegasus Ring

A Book of Poetry by
Charlotte Hart

The Pegasus Ring: A Book of Poetry by Charlotte
Hart

ISBN 978-0-6152-4539-3

Art Direction & Design by Virginia Garramone
Cover Photo by Charlotte Hart
Photograph of Susan by Franz Loewenherz on January 6, 2007
in Paris at La Coupole
Author Photo taken by Bob Hart

Cover Typeface - Bodoni SvtyTwo OS ITC TT & Book
Antiqua
Interior Typeface - Garamond

In Memory of Susan Jean Loewenherz

The Pegasus Ring
Given June 2004

S. J. I am giving this ring to you for a reason.

C.   You are generous and love me.

S. J. The ring is from Florence. It's a replica of an ancient Greek ring.

I'm giving it to you because you are a poet.

C.   Susan, I don't write poetry.

S. J. But, you will.

C H
2008

Table of Contents

3

Wednesday Night Light Dinner in July

A beautiful martini glass, crushed ice, lemon peal twisted, Turi Vodka.

Home roasted raw cashews and walnuts sprinkled with fleur d'sel

Eaten warm.

A teaspoon of Labna (sour cream textured pure white yogurt)

With a touch of ginger preserve on top adding a cool, tart, sweet dimension

To the warm nuts.

After waiting a few minutes and still feeling hungry, another teaspoon of Labna with a

tiny bit of ginger preserve on top.

After waiting another few minutes and still feeling a bit hungry another teaspoon of

Labna with a touch of ginger preserve on top.

That's it.

July 2004

Numbers 33:53
"And ye shall drive out the inhabitants of the land,
and dwell therein;
for unto you have I given the land to possess it."
33:56
"And it shall come to pass,
that as I thought to do unto them,
so will I do unto you."

Earth as Revelation

From and to the earth we travel in time
From our land to distant places

Land and identity
Land and book
Land and life

Our conversations linger and disappear in the air with our smiles.

The earth covers
Blood and gold
Jewels and
Memories

Time is giving us a chance to know our substance beyond the earth of being.

And in a warm, green, humid morning
Languorous in different thoughts
Unexpected revelation of a holy kind
Awakens.

July 17, 2004

Deuteronomy 31: 8:

The Lord, He it is that doth go before thee;

He will be with thee, He will not fail thee,

neither forsake thee;

fear not, neither be dismayed.

Hurricane

Native islanders who knew the ocean

    its dangers

        its currents

            and its power

made wise maps of cowry shells and wood to guide boats from island to island in safety.

Joshua's map was words of encouragement.

The eye of the hurricane is calm

but its arms are terror bringing fear and destruction.

Waiting. Hoping it won't come. Watching.

This hurricane of realization:

    capricious in mind fall with vast implications and dreaded truth

that bends and snaps tall trees of dreams

plans are swallowed in its roar

making armies of hopes into shards in raging winds.

We with our fragile maps and inherited ancient words

after the storm

    and deaths

        and disappointment

our fear alive

    our plans denuded like the mangrove and buttonwood

do what must be done.

September 11, 2004

He made him ride on the high places of the earth,

And he did eat the fruitage of the field;

And He made him to suck honey out of the crag,

And oil out of the flinty rock

Einstein thought that in observing an electron
and influencing its action it was not possible
to influence another distant electron to behave
the exact same way. He called that theory,
"Spooky action at a distance."
Quantum mechanics proved him wrong.

Spooky Action at a Distance

It is midnight
I'm not in pain
I lay in bed
Alert and awake
I observe
With closed eyes
My knowledge of
The meteor tumbling to earth
A train whistles in the distance
The crickets singing syncopated seconds
And your steady breathing
This is peace

I send my happiness from my safety up in a high arc
Past the hapless meteor about to burn
Across the seas
To create an identical happiness
In a different locality
An identical peace

I observe the earth by the Dead Sea

9

The lowest place
The humility of the earth
Dust and minerals
Crystals of salt slow dancing in the hot water

O Jerusalem!
In the heat of the day
Simultaneous locality
Of peace offered
From within my mind
I would enclose you in the womb
Of synchronicity
Of my own blessed moment
And hold the long breath
Of ancient ram's horn blast

From my distant locality
My measured hopes
Seek initiation of equal hopes
I lay in darkness communicating
Faster than the speed of light
Spinning identical
Electrons
In a magnetic passion
For peace
And then I sleep.

I awake.
O Jerusalem!
Zeinab Abu Salem
An eighteen-year old girl
Walked with her head scarf blowing
And then blew herself and two policemen
Into bloody parts and newsprint.

They'll taste no more of apricots and figs

Or

Sweet desert blossom honey harvested from the crag

Or

Green golden oil

At a distance

Both cause and effect

I observed peace

In great stillness

And faster than light

Shalom

Salem

Ended.

September 23, 2004

Vermeer and Eternity

Universal light through universal window
Ignored and lived every day of sun
Universal pouring
Universal milk
Glass bottles delivered to back doors in the fifties
Human hands squeezing down milk from bloated udders
Mechanical devices extracting milk
From cows in metal rows of pens
Milk
The milk of human kindness
Mother's milk
Mother pouring milk for me
Mom said,
"Drink your milk."
Sunshine and Mom
Nurturing and giving strength
And offering: milk, health and growth.
Feeling the milk you poured
In my bones
I watch you pouring.
Pouring stillness
Pouring calm
Pouring eternal pouring.
Streams of milk in endless flow,
Woman and milk are pouring and giving.
The light from the window warms.
You do not know that Dutch woman. She died hundreds of years ago.
But, because of Vermeer, she will never die. He has saved her moment
In the light of the window,
Her pouring milk
Her life in a moment
That

Was once in all eternity

And

Made it eternal.

You and I do not know her

But, we know her as never ending women pouring milk in the light of a window.

I have been a pouring woman

In the sunshine window of my own moments

And then

Though not saved in oil and pigment

By a genius of contemplation and skill

Was eternal too.

November 23, 2004

The Chateau and Barbara Gabor

We were at a chateau
Of great proportions
Ancient stones in curving modern lines
It was solid from earth to sky.
We were walking at the base
And you, looking at the sweeping vista around and below
 Said, "This is too much!"
And I said," Would you rather having only lived in Missouri?"
You began to walk down the sloping hill
Your back was straight
You were wearing a hat and a long dress
And you walked with dignity and care.
I began to follow
And realized that the gently sloping hill had been cunningly glazed with a slick of water
Flowing from an unseen source.
But though you were walking on water
There were no ripples or splashes
And I followed on the path.
In the distance, below the hill
The countryside was bucolic like a painting.
You turned at the edge of the walkway where the path curved
I saw you from afar
And you continued on and around the top of the hill
Walking tall.

December 8, 2004

Reenie in Black

I saw you shopping

You were in the corner of a store talking with a man

And you were trying on a plaid knee brace over black stockings.

He had boxes of expensive cigars on his top shelf

Which caught my eye

And there were shelves of books below.

You were to my left and another lady was to my right

And you mentioned the pie.

Ceremoniously you brought forth a piece and said, "Pear."

Then you took a long toothpick in one hand

And a piece of clear plastic wrap in the other

And cut, or shaved, a sliver of pie onto the clear plastic.

I tasted it. There was a touch of chocolate too.

I thought it might pair nicely with chestnut

Or possibly Pear William

But it was good as it was

And I kept the taste on my tongue like memory.

December 8, 2004

A Commercial

A white screen became the realization of water when a baby, surrounded by bubbles,

Swam into view and away

There was a moment of a green place with delighted laughter

And there were glimpses of promise and happiness.

A giant print out

A scan of all the scenes

Left the printer

And it lay there in bas-relief

Some places in its patchwork were fluffy clouds

And others were scenes

The one at the bottom

Was of three girls, two white and one brown

And the thought

Was of many choices

All good

And it left me with such a lovely and peaceful feeling of happiness

As though angels had come from the sea and the clouds and proven their presence through my printer.

December 8, 2004

Hospital Waiting

For B.

Incessant TV is the comforter of fear and loneliness.

The fan blades above the ceiling grate are

Throwing cold air on bacteria.

By the wall, white irises are curling in on themselves

Their glory was four days ago.

The fuchsia Phalaenopsis orchid presides over the bedside table clutter.

Shriveled carnations amid evergreens are in a vase by the sink.

I.V. monitor, wheel chair and walker are the landscape of this time.

"Thank you for being my friend," said the voice on the T.V.

We sat in chairs around the bed

While you slept.

Tomorrow is the surgery.

You will soon be well

And go home.

December 16, 2004

My Brother's Home

The tattered and faded Tibetan flags flapped suspended over the pool.

A mosaic of fallen leaves rests on the surface of the water and in random patterns on the bottom.

A white cat with no tail like an animal emanation of fossil Florida stone sauntered near the pool.

On the table in a tattered basket was an orchid struggling for life.

This is the home of my brother:

the Doctor of Salt

   flyer above the clouds like dragon creativity

     wrapped in chagrin

       listening to music in his memory

so intense that it touches his nerves in Prague while

it is

     slipped in its leather case in Coral Gables.

Marble and granite

   bromeliad and avocado

     little walking penis key

       and truffle oil.

Key code: "Pt195.09"

There is an immortal woman floating out of the open mouth of a daemon in his bedroom

   and islands wrapped in pink in the hall.

Complex brother,

who corresponds with your heart?

Who corresponds with your mind?

Your beloved children will give you like kind.

January 1, 2005

This Time

For B

I see how tired you are

I see how valiant

Infestation of plastic pill bottles, amber with white caps and labels

You look up

I think of you looking up with your dark hair blowing in the black and white photo of you in college.

I wash your short white hair

I brush your hair.

Your walker basket is filled with unopened mail

Your rubalite ring catches the afternoon sun in its still pink intensity.

Wheelchair folded

Waning chances for pleasure:

Soup from *Mango's,*

Perogies,

Nesim dorma,

Inexpensive mulch.

You who are the world

Sleeping so deeply that waking seems to you like

"Being put back in place"

A shock

Imobility

Sad pain.

Beautiful, beautiful beloved life

You gave like a torrent

Blessings profound

Religious outside of ritual

Generous and brilliant.

What can I do?

I fly to you

I cook to please

I garden away the desolate.

I shop.

We talk,

Don't go

Don't suffer

Let me help

Don't cry

Anything but good-by.

April 2005

The Keys Weren't Lost

Out by the side of the house
  by the palms
was where you buried the tightly closed jar.
  your hidden hoard
your mind adored
  your body absorbed
in a breath the change
  from place
    to edges removed
      time manageable
        eyes to lizards scampering by the aquamarine pool
gold painted nails
  Renaissance ring
    glinting in sunlight future
      a woman's privacy displayed in gold around your neck.
Oh generosity!
You used to like spinning 'till you dropped and now you like
  a delicious dinner, red French shoes and the boy growing in Basia's belly.
Capricious whims and pleasures
  how they package life like the gift it is.

April 21, 2005

O'Keefe and the Principal of Big

Looking

Looking again carefully

Seeing

Seeing clearly

Wanting others to see

What you see

So you told them in paint

Big

Really bigger than big

So that they would not ignore you

And see you and what you saw

The way you saw.

You saw your self really big

And

You painted flowers to tell it.

They believed you

And

You are.

April 21, 2005

An Aging Woman of Natural Beauty

If you are not competing with an idea of beauty

And you have made more right choices than wrong

And are not in pain most of the time and yet have known pain

And are thinking and wondering and still have room for hope and dreams

And cherish hearing the music of the past and of the present

And are shocked with delight

At the smallest things and the biggest things

Each sense awake, aware, awed

And you have friends

And you have people that love you that you love

And you feel the joy that sometimes wells up within

So intensely that you are the child you were long ago

But safer and more you than you were

Then you are beauty.

A blazing red-orange-yellow leaf dancing against a clear blue sky

In the fall wind breaks free from its branch.

April 26, 2005

Sunday Brunch for Lovers Sweet and Savory

Remembering my Oma Frieda's kitchen
I blended three eggs
Laid by chickens running around freely eating grain in the sunlight
With a half cup milk and a half cup flour
And let it rest.
I dotted Oma's black iron frying pan with three tablespoons of sweet butter
And poured the batter on top
Seeing little butter islands above the batter.

In another iron pan
Truffle oil
Like the first dots of a rain on porch furniture
Sizzled under fern fiddleheads
And thinly sliced white bulbs, rose stems and ribbony green tops of wild woodland
Ramps.
Two golden yokes were folded into whites
Beaten stiff and fluffy as the white cat-face cloud in the sky.
Half of the eggy comforter was placed
In another buttered iron pan
Topped with two slices of mild Halvarti cheese
The fiddleheads and ramps
And tucked in with the rest of the fluff.

While sweet and savory baked at 400°
For twenty minutes
Lemons were sliced
Powdered sugar readied
Apricot jam heated
Droste cocoa prepared with whipped cream
Black coffee poured.

This brunch was served in bed
Surrounded by newspaper

And enjoyed while looking out the balcony window

Over blooming wisteria bedecked trellis

Over plumb tree

Past apple blossoms

And

Ruddy Japanese maple, blue spruce, and tall birch bending in quiet affirmation.

The sun glowed and hid and glowed

Through dark and white clouds giving only glimpses of blue

To the voice of Pavarotti

And then,

The WFMT music of Boulez, Schubert and Larry Adler.

Savory cooked.

Sweet did the dishes.

May 15, 2005

We woke early
Sipped coffee
Saw faces
On TV
Of
Casualties.
Young faces of men and women
Serious in their military photos
Lost American children
Dead
Far away in Iraq and Afghanistan.

We drove south on I95
Cement, cars, trucks, palms.

The faculty processional
Procession of the Nobles
The Processional of the class of 2005
Joyful parents
Awkward eighteen-year-olds
Confident
Girls
All in white
Headed to Brown and Yale
Young men
Headed to Yale and Harvard
The Invocation
The chorus singing the alma mater
Video cameras
The introduction of the commencement speaker
Pride
The commencement address

Presentation of honors

And

Awards

Valedictory

And

Salutatory Cups

Salutatorian

Honor

Valedictory Address

Awarding of diplomas

Benediction

Recessional

A reception was held in the quadrangle.

May 27, 2005

Conversation with Michelle Waiting for Carryout at Jalisco

We went together to a junk shop she liked to go to that she called

The Boutique.

There were old lamps, kitsch paintings, used clothes and blankets, pressed glass

And at a counter in the front

There was jewelry.

I saw this ring,

Spreading my fingers,

The pink, pale purple, yellow and watery blue faceted colored glass in the ring sparkled.

Mom liked the ring. I asked the lady to let her try it on.

It fit!

I bought it for her for about twelve dollars.

She wore it a lot.

Although she owned many expensive rings,

Whenever she wore this ring

People commented on its beauty.

Yesterday she gave it back to me.

I turned my hand over to show the scotch tape that I'd wound around the back

Over and over

Until it formed

A tape cocoon.

Michelle said, "It fits."

May 31, 2005
Ft. Lauderdale, Fla.

I Don't Drink

A man at the wedding, a child psychiatrist with no children, spoke of just having finished the Iliad, told me, "I don't drink."

I said, "My son once sat next to another boy in high school until one day the boy wasn't in his seat because he had died in a car accident caused by drunk driving. My son didn't drink a sip of alcohol after that for three years."

He said, "When I was an emergency room doctor I used to see what alcohol did."

"What is it about alcohol you do not like beside misuse?" I sipped my glass of wine.

"The taste."

"The taste? Of sunlight on grapes and warm summer days saved in juicy memory?"

"I just don't like it."

"Cordials? Beer? Hard liquor? Even gin, which is hard, has fifteen or so many different botanicals. Each is blended and cannot be distingwished; but, together, they sing like a fine chorus."

"I don't like it."

"Maybe you're an ascetic."

"No, I am not," he said, looking at his half finished dessert.

I had another glass of wine.

"Maybe it's not the taste. Maybe it's the alcohol itself that you are uncomfortable with."

"Maybe."

"Personally, I couldn't give up the poetry of intoxication. Once my grandfather hosted a thirtieth birthday party for my Aunt Norma, who was feeling old. He went to the wine cellar and got a bottle of wine that was thirty years old and a bottle that was forty years old. He opened the thirty-year old bottle and everyone enjoyed it. Then he opened the forty-year old bottle. Norma exclaimed how much better the forty year-old bottle was."

"That's a nice story."

My husband and I danced. We laughed with the bride and groom and then returned to our table.

The fifty year old never married before medical doctor bride's eighty-year-old father beamed. The fifty-year-old symphony orchestra horn player turned lawyer groom's children, happy for their dad's joy, didn't think of the divorce. Musicians and doctors, lawyers and family, danced and drank and smiled and talked.

Healing married music and justice.
  Celebration view of Millennium Park from the *Cliff Dwellers Club*
    white lace heady, dancing champagne high
      I had another glass of wine, wedding cake, and coffee.

June 11, 2005

…"because our inheritance is fallen unto us on
this side of the Jordan eastward"
Numbers: 32:1-19

Inheritance

Trying to keep people together for holy purpose
    trying to keep family together for love
        holding together is a battle with freedom.

I see the earth dancing around in human bodies
        living land
with identity and personality
    one's body inherits.

Remember those with no freedom
    taken
        turned to smoke.

Who are those who step forward?
  They choose to serve
      and cross the Jordan of the mind.
The Israeli pioneers returned to their land of inheritance
  a tattered family with God's will flowing in their DNA
        XY disproportionately Cohens
      mitrocondrial shocks of origin
          people with identity enough to face battle.

Who are Reuben and Gad?
They choose freedom of outside lands
  diaspora identity
and might be lost
and might be happy.

Turning from sinful to builders

31

took time

births and deaths

    until the smile of this moment

        another son of Aaron is almost born

            but that identity will not be given to him.

And what of distracted angels

    who take the warm spark of a soul and throw it into the new breath body of an infant

        belonging to another family in another place?

            Two Chinese babies

                born in different cities

                    given up by their mothers

                        brought to the USA

                            now with Chinese and Hebrew names

                                will grow with blessings in their mouths

                                  a new inheritance

                                      sweeping them into the bundle of souls of

America and Israel.

Trying to keep together for holy purpose

and love

valuing the laws

valuing the people

valuing the land

miracle of caring.

Inheritance:

    turning away inheritance

        denied one's inheritance

            choosing inheritance

                being chosen for an inheritance:

Laughing and crying earth are we.

July 30, 2005,

Aquamarine

Glitter ring
Healing
Lake Michigan on an August morning

August 18, 2005

African Gray

There was a lady at work who had one of those really smart parrots that knew many words and could speak sentences. The parrot learned new words all the time and the lady who owned it tried to keep it stimulated because if parrots get board they pull out their feathers.

One day the lady put the parrot on her back porch. From that place it could watch people walking their dogs in the alley and hear snippets of conversation, car radios as the cars drove by, and the "L" train.

The parrot sat on its perch for a while watching and listening.

A flock of birds flew up from a tree, made a loop and landed on a garage roof. The parrot watched them go from the tree to its right to the roof on its left. The flock of birds flew up again, flying up high, the parrot watching, and they curved around in the air before landing back in the tree. This flying from tree to roof to tree to roof continued carefully observed by the parrot. The flock flew again into the air and the parrot said,

"Come here."

November 14, 2005

Another Launch

Caressed by mathematics
      algorithm streamers are twirling and twisting
            with e-confetti ordered not random in its falling
                the visualizer is like hot creamy chocolate
      enjoyed with R&B
           and South African Syrah.

Your kiss and smile are returned to me through the porthole of Lexapro.
First sky
      clear cobalt young ease with days stretching endless
Then ocean
      foaming bubbly green of suppressed laughter
sky
then ocean
      fill the circle as our ship lists.

No teak deck chairs, or legs wrapped in plaid wool blankets or uniformed mate with
tray of teacups steaming
      a confetti of pharmaceuticals accompanies another launch of our continued trying.

Our stationary journey is 3.5 or 4.0 on the treadmill monitor as we run through
Myanmar at the Levy Adult Center.

Spectral is our will on November brittle days. Breath hovers outside our lips
      knocked out of us by loss and time and temperature
      the commonness of aging that disappears on the horizon line of newly realized
limitations.

With no land in sight but with technology that indicates land is so near
             the i-Tunes song play count is 99
             and the words are, "my love has never died."
November 17, 2005

Dressed in New Times Roman

They are marching by
　dressed in New Times Roman
　　demonstrating their silent voices very well written.
Serious recognized writers:
　Masturbatory childhood homoerotic memories
　　Angry African American political
　　　Selfish daughter hurting her mother
　　　　Bitter lost passion
　　　　　Distributing ashes of the dead here and there.
　Dying to be read
they are serious recognized writers
some with one book or more.

　　　　　Readers left with voyeurism
　　　of dark alphabet cunningly ordered on parade
　　　　　turn to

　　　　　　　　　　　Joy
　　　　　laughing daughters, seatbelts fastened
　　　　　　　　　　Honor
　　　son with two tassels on the same mortarboard
　　　　　　　　　　　Grace
　　　　　　　　　falling softly
　　　　　　　　　Character
　　　　　　　　not doing it
　　　　　　　　　Wisdom

36

seeing the moment from a future moment

and choosing what would be best when this moment is long gone

Compassion

the center of a wheel of action to repair or help or lift up

Humor

heals. Laughter is an internal massage.

And Wit.

Give us wit!

Who gives a wit?

Anyway.

November 21, 2005

In a message dated 12/20/05 7:23:18 PM,
xOXOx1@hotmail.com writes:

poor choice of role model

http://www.cnn.com/2005/US/12/20/tookie.funeral.ap.ap/index.html?section=cnn_t
opstories
Several dozen gang members wearing blue attire
associated with Crips
gangs watched the funeral in the parking lot.
One who identified himself as "Killowatt the Third," age 33,
estimated there were 20 to 30 Crips-affiliated gangs there to honor Williams.
"That's my role model, man.
That's the CEO of the Crips," he said.

reply

He Kilt Fo Pepo Tweny Years Ago

street rif raf jesus martyer ta mosesless populas......a few chiltrens books do not
murtders erase. C

reply

"You're the Robert Browning of Rap" D

collage poem: Charlotte and David Hart e-mail
January 5, 2006

South Miami Hospital Waiting Room

The strangers are all alike
    hands clasped in prayer
        backs bowed
            all thinking of another.
Fear is here
dread too
but in the silence is laughter
    of brothers holding hands
        in the air
    before their feet touch
      the glittering lake.

Mom, with her bushel basket of tomatoes
    red, orange and green

The aria Nessim Dorma at the Met
Sweet sixteen whose
smiling dad offers the carnation corsage.

Black coffee. McDonalds. Guava pasteries
    and a vapor of things that were not said
      in English, in Spanish.

Snow falls on these memories and builds up in drifts of comfort
    in distant places. Prayers rise in coral, turquoise, bleached yellow, lime and rose-violet
  envelop each other
    rainbow of peace eminated by need in this sunny, hot Miami storm.

Surgeon's knife
    bleeding
      a smile
        children at home

waiting

kindness amongst strangers of clinched hands.

January 25, 2006

A Methodist Lady

At one time the Methodist Home was filled with ladies like Edna Ewohn

maiden ladies wearing suits with white hair pulled back or curled cut short,

retired teachers, librarians, church organ players.

Those ladies gave all their money to the Methodist home with the promise of being

taken care of the rest of their lives and buried.

Edna was the last of them all.

She once taught our children piano and she would stay for lunch.

After her heart surgery twenty years ago, she spoke of dying with her pastor, friends and

nursing home attendants. She was on the verge of "going" for twenty years.

But the last four times we saw her in Weiss Memorial Hospital, she was going.

She seemed to shrink. She gave me her two rings.

"I'm afraid. I'm afraid," she said.

And she went.

The funeral was at St. Boniface and the ashes of her dog were in the coffin by her feet

as she wished.

Stooped elderly ladies from church stood in a circle by the coffin.

There were three Methodist ministers at the chapel, door open, that freezing February

morning.

Edna's faith was spoken of. The promise of heaven and being in the presence of Jesus

was spoken of with reverence.

Then Edna's friend, Sherry, interrupted loudly,

"Edna didn't believe in God. She became an atheist."

The reverend stopped speaking and then continued her eulogy.

February 11, 2006

Teatro Museo Dali

North Florida
Florida Nord
bent ear
can't hear.

Like the soft clock
time slips away
a cold Coke down a parched throat.

February 22, 2006

Ancient words read then spoken, "Is the Lord among us or not?"

hung setaceous in the Saturday air

and a laminar flow of black flakes

ashes without fire came from the letters off the page

floating around the library and people

flakes of unspoken doubt.

A sprout of green grew from the center of my forehead

into my brain

and a single blue flower bloomed in my mind that instant.

"We can know if the Lord is among us or not. We should wait expectantly and the

answer will come to us differently and individually through our sense of smell."

There was embarrassed silence.

I waited that day, but it did not happen, only the glistening black ink lines of my

imagination dipped and swirled as they dried.

There were faces of serious young men and women in silence on Channel 11.

A golden dome was blown up.

Riots and bombs exploded.

We bought wine. Meals were eaten. There were phone calls. Short trips were taken and

small tasks finished. We walked in place. I remembered my mother and father often.

Full circle we sat in the Saturday library again, books open, reading the ancient words of

another week.

A woman next to me reached to a bowl of fruit, pealed a tangerine,

and I knew

through my sense of smell

the oil of tangerine was my affirmation.

February 28, 2006

43

Color

You in deep dull blue
admired my colors:
creamy mint, scrubs green,
peach, pale blue and sparks of red.

Go to Vogue Fabrics and find one-yard swatches
in colors that make you feel happy, astonished, comfortable, sexy, like someone else, or
more like yourself
whatever you like and wear them singly or together as scarves.

You need to be careful of relationships and money; but, with color you can be
extravagant and reckless
and nothing bad will happen.
You said you were inspired to try.
There are very few circumstances that one can be reckless and safe.

Color is reckless and still safe
unless you're in the wrong neighborhood.

April 23, 2006

44

La Spezia Four O'Clocks and Love for My Sister Susan

We walked across the beach and sat on the sand.

The October afternoon was warm and the sun was setting.

Mediterranean waves rolled in steady Verdi rhythm.

A woman walked ankle deep, lightly splashing, outlined in light,

her hair blowing from under her hat.

A father walked by with a baby strapped to his chest.

Sonat fell asleep on the sand. We leaned back on our elbows.

Light glittered on the waves. Ships were distant on the horizon.

We sat together in acceptance for a time long enough.

Two little dogs, jumping and barking woke Sonat.

We slowly got up to leave. We walked back in no hurry.

I saw the yellow four o'clocks growing wild at the end of the beach and collected their
seeds.

This warm April afternoon I missed you and needed your voice.

You returned my call.

After we talked I told you,

"To commemorate this call I will plant the four o'clock seeds. They stayed in my change
purse since that day at the beach."

"Good," you said,

"Then they will be blooming when I get there in September."

April 25, 2006

Rousseau of Words

Africa day1
I am in the Sossusvlei dunes
Walking on diamonds
Dazzled by stars.

Africa day2
Time is different in Damaraland
where it is the elephant's steps that bring day to night
oryx elude and springbok surprise.

Darkness here has warm breath.
The campfire flames
flying swarms hum.

Dark skinned Namabians walking like waves of heat
whose common gestures
"Hello"
"Good-by"
take on mystic meaning and grace.

An ostrich feather falls and brings thought back to New Orleans.
African American people on rooftops in anguish in the Superdome of desperation
heat and stench,
looting, dying
and being denied.

The sunrise and smoldering fires
now reflect on still flooded streets.

Africa day3
Etosha Leopard
      speed of mind

spots and need
　　　　inspiring flight.
Running deer
　　zebra stripes and fear
　　　　a wildabeest to bloody feast.

Ongava Lodge
chilled white Hamilton Russell Chardonnay 1998, Walker Bay
in a glass held up to the sunset
a raptor circles and seems to rise from the wine.

A distant lion roars in this dry season
by precious water hole
and from within me comes a roar
from the tips of my fingers
from the souls of my feet
the crown of my head
and the depth of my stomach
a soundless roar
　　　leaving my mouth
　　　　　into the African heat
　　　　　　　and the roar says,
　　　　　　　　　"Alive."
Africa day4
Seductively curving
the Zambezi River
flowing to the edge
　　foamy white ribbon of water
　　　　spray disappearing into humidity
　　　　　　unstopped fall
slender white arm of the river
　　Victoria's arm
　　　　reaching down into the heart of Africa.

Slender dark arms of the people

    reaching up into the foaming spray

      wet hands to faces

        cooling water

on dark necks

  balm

    of a moment under the Acacia trees.

Evanston day5

I wanted to go into Africa

  but couldn't leave Evanston, Illinois.

Africa came out of me

  experienced in poems.

May 18, 2006

Osip Mandelstam

I knew you were looking for me.

    Was it the time I was covered with bees

        their wings and fuzzy bodies skimming on my cheeks, forehead and bare arms?

From the first phrase I recognized you,

    you called to me 'armed with the vision of slender wasps'

        but I was not born then.

You were not at St. Isaacs in St. Petersburg. I only saw the malachite columns.

Now that I have found you

    you are gone.

We both realized it was not fleshy knowing that is ours.

Your words have thrown off their Leningrad coat

    and trust you with me in Chicago.

Your thoughts reached me as you knew they would, Crooked Street.

I yearn for and call and cast my dancing lines to another unborn

    who will know me instantly

        as I knew you.

May 22, 2006

Mid-Summer

Clinging to the last of July
one hundred degrees
drooping hydrangeas
slow motion then still
my will.

July 31, 2006

3:19 A.M.

Everything is whole.

Nothing is finished.

The inside grows out.

August crickets repeat

a power fugue.

August 9, 2006

Es Wird Weider

It Will be Good Again

You and I know the cold late October rain
   the Berlin of the soul,
graffiti sadness that covers the inner walls of all thoughts.

My love lay in bed, clinching his jaws in fear
his panic left me breathless
   helpless
      while I mourned.

You, sister in deep mother loss,
   faced your own fear and pain
      cold chemo and burning radiation.
         Now you rest in Venice and recover.

Not yet gone a year
   Mom called my name and told me she needed me
      and demanded," Come here!"
What could I do but wake up?

In that chilled gray rain, the year falling in brown leaves, bankrupt hope changed from
dollars to Euros
   off balance as I stepped in puddles that dripped in my mind unlike nature
      I drew nothing solid no dimension
until
   I walked across a German phrase stenciled on wet pavement
      and Sonat, who cures the world, translated the hope it held.

            "Es Wird Weider,"
            "It Will Be Good Again."

Now it is June.
   Mom is still gone

but in everything I touch and smell and see and taste and hear

   she is present in my enjoyment

      with a growing group of the beloved also not here.

He smiles again. I love it when the rhythm changes. Joy. Syncopation.

Now there is perfume filled air from sweet fluffy pink peonies.

   They promise prosperity.

   A new life is growing.

Time has put those other things back there.

   See the white marble topped mountain

      and your summer cloud of mind gliding Venetian smooth

         unseen birds sing in Italian as morning sunlight warms your dreams.

In August we'll eat grilled sweet corn on the cob together

   swim in the mystic lake

      show marble, granite, ink and paper that remember our touch and thought

         to people who walk and pause

            in the U.S.A.

August 9, 2006

The Song

In memory of Dennis Joseph Glynn Jr. 1976-2006

He came back from New York defeated,

his elegant fashion designs un-chosen.

In August he tried.

A bolt of red silk rolled away from him and he was afraid.

I walked up three flights of stairs and hugged him in the doorway, his wrist, wrapped.

"Call day or night."

"I will. I will"

Pills, other pills, therapy and therapy,

he left Oona's birthday party early.

Too tired and sick

he missed New Year's dinner for the first time.

In March, in a whisper, Oona told me that he did it

  driving without moving

    the door was closed

      all of us disappeared

        with his breath.

Den's charcoal drawings, lost dusty laughter, and rosy-cheeked plans

got the attention of an angel. He sang for him in barely audible, ethereal tones

of bruised coral, darkest cobalt blue, black, silver, iridescent pearl, and gold.

Almost obscured by the sound of millions of dreams folded into electrical combinations

that scratched each other unseen in breathless tumble

  the majestic song gave hope of finer worlds

    where burdens would not be so great.

Amidst sustained static, the angel's voice continued with musical notes of fabrics:

tweed and tulle, silk and knobby wool, cotton, rayon, spider's web.

Indistinguishable voices droned in unintelligible conversation.

They didn't need more food; there were trays and trays of tears.

I took my glasses off, not to see him on sateen.

August 9, 2006

Approval

The dark eyed nursing mother, head covered with a blue flowered scarf,
pulled her nipple from sucking tongue, tattoos showing for an instant,
and placed the infant in her seven year old daughter's arms as
her three other young children played on the floor.
She turned to stir a pot of vegetables
and lifted the lid on the rice pot.
A steam cloud escaped.

Her husband entered the kitchen, proud and smiling.
He bragged to the other man, wearing a bomb vest,
"My wife too is ready to dress in bombs and achieve honor in death."
She blushed with pride. She felt her unborn kick within.

August 15, 2006

Behold the Hidden

The earth falls away and a deep purple-red beet comes out with a tug

Golden urine streams from the body

The sky gives up its stones

An ax hits a stone and a live frog jumps out

All the words from all the mouths

Wait for ears

September 28, 2006

Judaism, Christianity, Islam

Jews had twelve tribes.

Jews have 613 electrical sparks of positive and negative laws

that pulse in their numbers and names: daled'n aleph.

The Law of Return circles in time and space and ends to begin in Israel.

Gafilta seasons of klesmer and candles, studying outside walls,

curious watchers, distinct voices, great gifts and givers,

stiff necked in argument with self, each other, and God.

Red, blue and purple threads from the sanctuary flow with sferic crackle,

the remnant not burned is still electrifying souls on earth.

Nobels, law, business, Hollywood glamour, music, scholarship, research: the talking ass

reverberates, dwelling in vellum scroll, less than one percent of everywhere,

charged to labor, to repair the world, to be worthy of breath. Artistic and technical

miracles: water no longer asunder, no pillor of fire, no pillor of smoke.

Marvelous daily life, compassion and intelligence schooled in rigorous passion for work,

protecting the seventh day with devotion.

No right to exist. Hated.

Christians had

twelve apostles.

Christians have

everlasting life and

baptismal certainty.

Virgin mother and mild child face eternal fate in Renaissance beguiled oil paint.

Convents of love and secreted mysteries, transformations in crutches abandoned cave.

Messiah donkey: angels lifting the squalid to cleanliness of body and soul and love.

Miracles.

Glory.

Relics.

Saints.

Gold

embroidered

satin.

Splendor

with

humility,

children and

childless

devotion,

emotional

promise

of

Western

Identity.

Gospel

of

eternal

life.

Singing swaying church straw hats, kings and queens: righteous chess of equal balance
held in chocolate fingers and white hesitance. City, suburb, highway and hidden place
self lurking like taste of shame now given sunlight bright ride in youth yearned ruby
smooth shined fenders.

Islam had twelve tribes.

Islam has land, oil and power.

Hot mint tea pours into the bottom of the etched glass.

Chaos liquid swirls and rises, gives its perfume and meets lips at the edge. Inhale the
hanging gardens of Babylon, burqa lingering jasmine, madira steaming for guests.

Mecca changed the direction of the divine to black stone and Zamzam waters.

The Perfume of Iraq was found in a hole.

Surging masses some trampled in worship visit of a lifetime for sultan and the poor.

Arabian stallion, Persian ghazal poetry and miniature painted portals to love and
luscious fruiting worlds in vast water hating dust: Ishmael's tents became Burg al Arab,
the tallest tent, luxury tent of tents, submission to wealth, exhilaration of power.

Hagar's validation: pumping hearts, great gigabarrels people, pumping black gold, light
sweet crude, passionate fists, self flagellation, blood of religious certainty flowing in
their children.

Laugh and laugh and laugh: hospitality eternally extended,
suicidal children returned to calm,
Isfahan, Kilim, silk Qum, Tabriz
billions of knots and fringes.

Triune of blood, the future physics of unlikely peace,
offer each other gracious sensual mathematics.
Together, enjoy something delicious to eat, saliva ecstatic, for common ancestor's sake.
Listen! Earned admiration of each other's children with
date, fig and pomegranate praise for the future.
Why so much transliteration and interpretation
of text and ties, bombs and lies?
Now
seize a new breath with collective pink lungs powerful and
rejoice in each other,
help each other,
our family.

October 20, 2006.

Laugh in Black and White

Collage Poem with Hafiz

How did the rose ever open its heart
rheostat slowly stronger yellow flushed with pink
and give to this world
minutes of green breath in freezing air
its crystalline aroma of fragile beauty?

Waning sunlight warmth discretely shown on the hail battered,
bright glow teacher not scorning attempt,
knowing the nucleus in every cell would be
too frightened.

Sing: people join with surfacing whales and howling wolves
our starving world needs
to fight the moon for food.

Laugh in black and white
because that is stumbling uncertainty
the purest sound.

When the words stop: and you can endure the silence only with fire or smoke or
Occam's razor cutting the past that
reveals your heart's pain of emptiness,
that great wrenching-sweet longing:

That is the time to try and listen
to what the Beloved's eyes
most want to say, understanding eyes
somewhere in the imagination of lost hope.

Admit something: need makes everyone look like the one.
Everyone you see: in crowds at the airport, in the blur of passing car glances, and when
you put the wine glass down. In a group of women, you smell vetivert perfume of your

mother's youth when she held you up to see the lions. The yearned for is identified in a waitress' pancake random smile. Fulfilled desire is promised by library book distracted glance.

And to each, your eyes say,

"Love me."

You are answered in your blood
by the God who only knows four words
and keeps repeating them, saying:
"Come dance with Me."
You are unable to refuse.

October 24, 2006

Bring **B**ali back to its sweet
innocent pagan splendor
of fruit and flower offerings
outside doors in
the morning
and artists of
wood carving
painting
silver work
Gamalin music
and dance.
Ancient fight
between good
and evil I have
joined. I going to
suck terrorists off the map
and take the stand in Eden.
Bali will suffer no more.
The Boogey men with black sails
and black thought
hateful crimes against
unkown innocents their
al Quaida arrogance
blasting bodies and hopes
into tears. No! That's over!
Prayer of the love of life:
snakes of Southeast Asia
I will kill your energy.
It is my hatred of your
clove scented cigarette actions
that my will and
deeds now address,

running into battle like

American civil war soldiers,

a swig of whiskey before

limbs were

sawed off.

October 28, 2006

The Art of Sleep

4:43:17 A.M.

Silence
the essential canvas primed in white rabbits
no longer hopping
lasts Warhal time

Jackson thoughts
Pollock the day with memories splashing splattering thin and
chaotic
layered in webs of emotional

pills or booze
Won't snooze me kitsch
or learn calm great
with this tossing impasto

Under comforter
not comforted
drinking Hopper night coffee
black to dawn

solace rest many colored
Chagall dreams
do not come to my
Dali-less waiting

my impression
of this night ballet I am every Degas dancer
at angled bed barre
stretching legs adjusting costume curving arm

you rococo softly

what rijns my rest?

5:55:50 A.M.
November 3, 2006

Attention: the Flavor of Carmel not the Texture of Tacks

fear no more web M.D. a place refuse to go
looking for death in headache or stiff neck
arcane obscure pussy growths and terminal red patches

fear no more web news
seeing world war in exploding fanatics or
lightless Korean North night-scape
unseen Iranian deep desert tunnels and enriched uranium stashes

now narrow sight to the Rollaflex double lenses
one open always seeing and
one closing for an instant
saving
this moment you choose to see

and what do you choose to see
in all the life breath choices you have that compose this music of yours
the orchestra in its grandeur
the silence of contemplation
a human voice
a harmonica

practice feeding Shrödinger's calico cat
and eat a few more spoons of warmth at each meal
allow the snow to enlarge so that individual flakes
awe like the black dot Mercury passing slowly across the face of the sun
insignificant Wednesday significant events observed
those change the tenor of everything

November 9, 2006

snaps and hiss

sparks and stillness

facing each other with hands on chins

looking down at the board

her hand hovers

lifts the queen and places her with soft

wood on wood sound on a square

he said, "irritating" to himself

and moved a pawn

the fire sssssed with intermittent dots and dashes

and I sat and watched

full of scrambled eggs with feta and artichokes

and warm plum torte

this Sunday morning

coffee of calm.

November 12, 2006

What Kind of Cowboy am I?

Un-self-conscious power
working as a team we corral them
the mooing, baahing, a-ing, e-ing, eye-ing, oh!-ing and you-ing
on snow white field leaving no unnecessary tracks
consummate consonants nestled in sound units
ready for the kill.
Cowboys of language lariats, O, I am masculine now!
I could stick an exclamation mark in the middle
of the last sentence if I felt like it.

November 12, 2006

The Relation of Deed to Blood

A horrible wrong
ignorantly committed
flows as an absence
deep in the blood throughout the living body
and was once called a sin.

This chilly hidden record of an act or word that has
with out knowledge of effect
left the body
a record of hurtful action that escaped
without awareness and entered the world
and diminished other life
and
life within.

The unrealized absence reaches every organ
fleshy centers of command
mystic powers unique
circulating in each memory capillary
hidden.

A shock!
Electric the realization of personal responsibility
heating blood
and burning as it flows with regret
burning away absence in every vein
through the heart and brain and liver and kidneys.

Massive stupidity
like a perfect bullock

that was the human state of being while committing the fault
now with realization and regret for the event
is killed.
Flowing blood with human form in new acts
touches each direction of the world
the horns of the compass
repentance in active attempt to transform harm.

Cleansing fire in blood
how different than murderous, ignorant bloody fire
it is the spirit of contrition
escaping the body
smokey laminar yearning for what is holy
that is the sweet savor
and it pleases
what was once known as God.

Even now
this moment
with fiery blood
peaceful transformation of ignorant wrong
draws near.

November 17, 2006

Calm Mix

shuffle of

numbers, letters

faces and time

give this sunrise birthing day

reason

and

November 24, 2006

After I told you about Baron

How discreet of you
when seeing my mind unhinged
rambling from ponies to bowed peonies
you made no comment.
I was stumbling subjects unrelated
disconnected thought from thought
that is one thing death does
it makes the mind like a fist unfolding
releasing a handful of feathers

November 30, 2006

Bob once told me

If you fly with eagles

Don't expect the admiration of turtles.

Jerry's stepdaughter was like a great blue heron.

Betsy's got all her planets in Scorpio.

Susan's cat is Jazz.

Baron is gone.

December 3, 2006

A Snow Storm Through Florida Eyes

For Jim

How profound a turn of mind

from perception of gloat to sunshine invitation,

hibiscus welcome being best!

Sunny and sweet that

daytime game show phrase,

"Come on down!"

Warm Florida heart

and flamingo days

welcome all

who

cloaked in freezing white

watch school closings stream on the bottom of their screens

and hear radio storm chatter while cars skid and coats are pulled around

figures hunched walking against wet sleet.

Mild Florida,

how affirmative and gentle your December days,

how welcome, the reverie of sitting with you by your pool.

December 3, 2006

The Myanmar Part of Me

Bare feet on hot stone under golden splendor
Shwedagon Pagoda
three hundred and two feet into the sky to
welcome Buddha's hair.
Many Buddhas housed in row house shrines
offerings of fruit, flowers and soda with inserted straw
all the Buddahs met my eyes with Yangon calm.
Buddha, sacred of I don't care
I won't care
it will take care of itself
its not even there.

I *was* once there
temple dogs sleeping
under gold and glittering green mirrors
turquoise and cobalt, red, fiery orange and mercury clear
jeweled mirror mosaics dancing peacocks reflecting the transitory
with colored light and theme park design of emptiness as all.
Face to face with anti-matter and my mother-all-matter
I was luxuriant witness in the experience
as it slipped Gautama away
I care
carried in cunningly designed silver purse with holes.
What can I do with what happened
a waking fulfilled dream
a small jade stone I have as proof.

He told me
That is Sweetwater
they torture people there.
Oh, you mean in the past.
No, now they do it.

He told me

We have people that can turn into tiger.

I told him that we have people that turn into crows.

He nodded knowingly.

Past sultry acres of vetiver in the rain

Rutted road to Mandalay echoes Sinatra song

road of overloaded rusted trucks with men pressed tight together inside and standing on

dashboards in sopping wet longyi, their fingers clinging to open windows,

and six or seven crouched on the top

trucks of clinging men.

On the side of the road, fires built under palm huts,

stripped men waving their cloth to dry it by the flames

this was the road into wordlessness.

Poisonous snakes slithered in the tall grass.

Women with burled teak brown faces

decorated with dots and lines of cracking white cream mixed with sandalwood dust

for beauty

gazed up in sweltering undulate air.

Pagu stupa studded with precious stones the size of my fist

the wish fulfilling place of torments and poverty

pilgrims who look to supine wealth for what they will be when they let go.

Buddha is reclining, mystic lines on the bottom of his feet.

Andaman mirror gates reflecting what? The flash of light is too quick.

Peaceful phosphenes behind my closed eyes behind my

eyes open over the Pacific watching glittering flocks of sparks outside the window in

darkness.

Quiet returning to Chicago

like that

and
never telling
all these years
until now
and
why tell?
Tell whom?
Buddah.

My mother suffered with every step and I tried to help her in every way.

Eight white gloved uniformed Strand bells rang with applause and cheers and waved good by as we were driven to the Ocean Pearl with a circle of pigeon blood rubies.

December 9, 2006

When I was in the Russian Circus Before the Wall Came Down

E. was lifted up in the spotlight on a flight wire of romance little girls with pink gauze bows and their families and the audience women, puffy from fifty and fat with sixty and dry from seventy looked up and saw him fly gently into the Tschykovsky air like a Greek god, with only a white cloth around his passion he changed the old to young and lifted my young innocence out of its raped despair. Around and around above the ring he flew slowly he descended until he put one foot down and then the other and the spot light went out.

M. wore a red nose and colorful patches and large green shoes. He was filled with homemade vodka that he kept in jars with a thin curl of potato peal floating; and, sometimes when he didn't have enough vodka, he was filled with the alcohol of after-shave, which didn't taste as good. Without his make-up, he looked like his brown bear, stiff brown hair, small brown eyes and big stooped shoulders. Mouth hanging slightly open like it had been hit or like he had something that stunned him or like he didn't have enough breath. His bear could balance on a ball. He could dance. So could M. They were real friends. They were like brothers.

A. was a gypsy. He was an artist of stealing! He smiled and went out into the audience while the orchestra played a cheerful polka. He shook hands with the strangers. He tipped his hat. He showed respect! Up and down the isles he ran cheerfully meeting the audience. Back on the stage he called out in Russian, and Polish and English and German and Japanese, "Where are your watches?" In every isle there were missing Rolexs and Omegas, Tag Hauers, Brightlings and Patique Philipes along with the nameless others. A. knew where the good ones were! When the empty wrists were upset enough he calmed them all down by going directly to each returning the correct watch. He never mixed them up. A real artist: memorable, concentration, quality of style, timing, original!

All the girls in the chorus were pretty. We all studied ballet; but, weren't good enough for the Bolshoi or Kirov. Some of us had connections so we got into the chorus that way and some of us were pretty good, and there were two girls that were married into the circus to trapeze men. It wasn't good to have a baby. Your job would be gone. We got to wear better clothes on stage than in our lives and we danced like friends but we were enemies: jealous peas in a can. We were the sweet smiling cold dancers of hate. People fell in love with us. About half of the chorus got marred each year and left, pealing away from the stage like our dancing routine: one after the other.

G. with her auburn hair and her handsome husband, K., had the most lovely act. She wore beautiful long elegant evening gowns and he wore a top hat and tales. They danced the waltz in a spotlight. First she had a red gown and long red gloves with a red feather in her hair. K., never missing a beat, lifted a hoop over her head and opened his hand allowing black silk to fall from the hoop and cover G. He dropped the silk funnel immediately as they were dancing and as it fell she no longer had a red feather, she was wearing a black sequined hat, jewels, black long gloves and black formal gown! They kept dancing and he threw a handful of glitter up above her head and as it fell, their waltz never interrupted, she was wearing a crown, gold gown and gloves and, in a puff of smoke while they danced she appeared in a necklace of big pearls, a white gown and shoes and then in a shower of leaves she wore green velvet. We saw them waltz through many balls in minutes. They danced a lifetime. They never grew old. She had beautiful gowns. They kept dancing. That was love!

White nights in Moscow with mashed potato clouds dusk at eleven met us after the show. Tight-rope-walkers walked home. The conductor decided whom he would go home with. Chains of light bulbs were strung across the streets in shapes of stars, scaffolds held up churches and crumbling homes of old time rich. I hated to think of waiting in line in the morning to buy sox. I had a hope to go to America someday. Everything was good there. I would look out in the audience during the shows and search. There, my other mother, who was waiting for me, who had my passport, who loved me and was going back to the hotel with me; and, then we were going to leave together. In America we would shop together at full shelves of bread and even have peaches in winter. June in Moscow made me shiver.

December 11, 2006

B.

Dear sauturne of every good thing that ever happened to me
Mother of my great fullness and companion to the unsullied buffet
I carry you with me as you carried me
You are the flame of my creativity.

December 12, 2006

Burning

My father dressed in a summer blazer
Mother, under her wide brimmed hat
and the four of us in tow, escorted down the wide white stone steps
of the Repulse Bay Club to a table in the sun.
That Hong Kong afternoon, he ordered a Pimms Cup #1 for me
the eldest, sixteen years old, dressed in white.
I sipped and smelled the cool mint, tasted the icy cucumber and felt like a woman,
a hot grown woman whom men would desire,
the heady power of a girl's first Pimms.
Many years later the club burned.

Brataslava's paprika sagadin goulash
phallic thick candle burning in the middle of the table
your contests of eating hot peppers with Horst
the women, deciding who would father their children between sips of Schlivovitz liquid
plums of fiery young plans and steaming Palacsinta filled with apricot preserves
hot, hot, hot fruit in the winter version of summer.
We walked out into the snow.
There was work on a screenplay. We went places.
Then we didn't see Horst anymore.
Years later, I saw him. It was noon and we walked up to each other and said, hello.
I looked into his eyes and we stood there a long minute before saying good-by.
A snowy morning ten years later, I turned on the T.V.
A wrecked car was engulfed in flames. The announcer gave the name of the driver and
said that the car had been going over eighty miles an hour.
Horst, trapped inside, died in the flames.

I looked over the edge of the ship and there was Krackatoah
blunt, black smoking reminder of its explosive year. It sat in the Java Sea sullenly
steaming next to a young volcano rising near: Son of Krackatoa.
People used to take a launch over there. They would climb the sides of Krackatoa and
melt the bottoms of their gym shoes on the hot ash.

The legend of the phoenix rising from the ashes came from a bird nesting on the volcano's side, the heat warming her nest.
Serena's department store in Jakarta, which years later burned to the ground, had floors of treasures: batiks, ikat, wood carvings, metalwork, gold and silver jewelry lovely results of time spent in the hands of souls making art from the earth.
I bought a wood carving of a phoenix.

Rose and Henrick along with some deny
six million Jewish families billions do not
speak of it now
had everything they owned taken from them
or recognize it
lead naked to gas chambers
burned
not personal
vast.
After it was over, people said they didn't know
even the people who lived and worked and went to school so near that
ashes fell on them
entered their breath
and their food.

Passions, burning places, flames of accidents,
fiery volcanic earth
feverish hatred
holocaust of the global mind
brush fires of the news
time, an airy wall, spares from the burning, and then does not.

The sun in explosive grace sent a flaming arm into space
past the messenger
past 900 degree Venus
to Earth.
It reached black sky over Wausau, Wisconsin

as Jerry and I drove North

the lightless pine lined deer dangerous highway

Six flowing, sparkling columns of green light and one red

appeared from the tops of the pines to the crown of the sky in the darkness before us.

Electrical light poured, flowed and sparkled.

"Do you know what you're seeing?" Jerry asked.

To my dumbfounded silence, "That is the Northern Lights."

The next night a large group of friends who had lived in the North Woods all their lives

spoke of the lights, none of the people had ever seen the Aurora Borealis.

Immense burning must be more difficult to see.

And what is of more gravitas than the burning of six million innocent souls? What is

more essentially important to human life than the sun?

Some would say religion.

Not omniscient not omnipotent the stories that have inspired global good and evil

inner burning flames that cling to generations fanned by mothers and social forces

identity

crackling and consuming other identity

the unseen burning

only halos and auras.

December 17, 2006

Controlling the Situation

Quick turn of head rigid blunt cut swinging
smile flashed teeth white smile over.
She moved his coffee cup to a slightly different place on the table
her better place decisions correct.

December 19, 2006

"I'll call when I get there."

That without a heavy foot would be five hours.

Wave good by

college sticker

her girl friend waves.

Back to drawing black and white lines with breath, the music takes a bite out of time.

Stiff back after six hours bent, I unfold slowly and press the silence button.

Like waking up, I slowly think of something else and it is the call.

No call. I wait. I call.

I call and leave a message.

Later, I call and leave a message with a too cheerful tone.

I wait.

I look at the time. I mention that there has been no call. We say that it's fine. I begin to feel emptiness filling me, and fear filling the emptiness.

I cannot find comfort, and walk aimlessly and begin putting things away.

Anger creates stormy mental dialogues with her in the silent room.

Montages of horrible possibilities need to be rejected as they waking dreams appear.

This is not like her.

I call again and leave a frightened please call plea.

I cannot put my mind anywhere but on the phone and wait consumed with dread and tell myself that all is well. I cannot eat.

Unable to distract myself

I pray.

I call her friend.

He has not seen them.

It has been seven hours. I'm ready to call the police.

She calls.

"Hi, Mom."

Wherewereyouwhydidn'tyoucallI'vebeenso

afraid.

"We went out to dinner."

December 22, 2006

Where am I?

Without a soundtrack
unfettered by notes for sale
walking unplugged
no clarifying tune for mind to dance
no decoration of time by colors of rhythm
heart beat bare
you are there.

December 25, 2006

Trope of leaning, sunlight warm

trope of tune, moon cool

trope of words, thimblerig clever

using three cups

hiding figurative five senses under one

and guessing wrong.

December 29, 2006

12/31/06 12:27:31 A.M.

Frivolous stories of strangers

in sensational disposable format

lay next to a small Calvino book and candlewax spilled and dried near flickering votives

chocolate truffles and chess board mid game

two Macs folded shut

apricot schnapps from Austria

beer bottles and open cans of diet coke

the coffee table landscape beginning the last day of this year.

December 31, 2006

Close Family

Fire in the fireplace

family sitting on couches together

baby sleeping on a pillow on his dad's lap

cookies, cans of soda water, un-popped popcorn kernels in the bottom of blue bowls

five lap tops open

Apples glowing.

8:43 P.M.
January 1, 2007

89

Safad

I was mistaken for a nun

possibly because of the scarf that I wore on my head tied under the triangle

hiding my hair

possibly because I was at your service

and without being asked

cared for you.

But like a bride of god who serves and feels divine reciprocity

as I lifted your bags and carried your documents and straightened the chair and guided

your sitting and brought you a glass of water

you were allowing me the chance to do so.

We saw the earth cut away into three thousand years of history.

I planted two saplings, one for each of us.

In the bright heat, we walked up a twig ramp into an ancient olive tree

and sat in the branches as the prodigy played the shiny black piano amongst the leaves

and ripening fruit olive notes.

Together we entered Safad, the mystic city, you walking with two canes and filled with a

diamond dense core of skepticism.

I was young and old.

The sky pulled me up into its lapis calm and held me dry and transparent

then let me fall into my shoes.

In the court yard, carved into a stone tablet, was a hand holding an eye.

Painted on another stone tablet was a blue hand. There was a pump, a large glass

generator; a rusty coffee can filled with a ragged blooming red geranium.

Above a locked wrought iron gate were the hand written words *private home* in English

and in Hebrew.

The air was hot and still.

I looked up.

There above the building was a growing human fetus in the air

held to the private home by its pulsing umbilical cord and as I shifted my eyes slightly to the right I saw the ancient body, white and dead

floating above the private home.

January 2, 2007

This is an unusual rain

it's drops touch specific points

now I am not now

becoming blurr

washed to when

I wore seal's fur.

January 12, 2007

II Bad: How an Element Can Be Ruined

The ferry from the Chicago Yacht Club, now landfill,
loaded with vodka, gin, almond stuffed olives, Bremner's wafers, and cheeses
in the arms of cheerful father-adulterers wearing Sperry Topsiders
yachting afternoon with a daughter.

Chicago horizon up and down choppy receding
dials registering, wheel turned
men's drinks in hands ice clinking
convivial laughter escaping weekly control
headed to hot July summer out of contact distance
beyond water filtration lake palace and reach.

Land vanished sinking earth in toothy lake
followed by tips of famous buildings
Palmolive, Lake Shore Drive apartments kissing the lower back of Oak Street Beach,
Edgewater Beach Hotel gone
drowning in the law of horizon
succumbing to heaves and dips panting lake and change.

The motor in monotonous drone continued until water everywhere
screams of gulls, fresh pouring, fresh ice, motor off, men's shirts off
settled back sunlight deck chairs with alcohol of private conversation.

She read in the cabin of teenage angst, sat on the bow
mood of the lake changed
smooth and glassy swells infrequent large enough to seem flat
rocking gently hypnotically surrounded by body temperature
heat forgetful lulling.

"Why don't you take a swim?" offhand out loud thought
to garner more privacy to entertain the listless daughter by the rail.
Down the ladder into the warm lake

dry wet
release
swim.

Immense sky without clouds rolling glare cutting haze
floating in soft water looking up at nothing seeing emptiness disquiet turned to swim
eyes open looking down no resolution in lake dark Payne's gray depth
unseen fishes, eels, rotting sunken boats,
old bottle glass white green amber tumbled smooth.

Silky caress warm water
splashing disturbance of kicking feet
dipping under water totally engulfed
exhale into still air while wipeing eyes
not seeing the yacht

the size of her thumb distant unanchored
drifting in milky haze deeply breathing lake
shouting first of many fruitless calls
fearful resolve began to swim.

Counting strokes breaths kicks
looking up to know the hidden black undertow
sucking the hull away from grasp
hand over body legs kicking knowledge
"I should have known I knew Reach it or drown."

Heart beating inner motor body need
water skimming calling choking coughing cold
kicking in element unheeding of dread no wave of support to flow desperation to goal
shouting veins pulsing pink neck
got the attention of her father, his back to her, still deck chair drinking.
he shifted slightly around, raised his glass, a toast to her in the air
and turned his back.

94

Lake Michigan mood becoming rough wind blew unknown sound
trough and height of waves building anger falling hopeless
the swimmer eking out motion from floundering strength
reached the rising and falling ladder
hand slipped ladder lifted up to taunting sky
ladder lowering lifted on wave grasped by both hands
limp body raised against rolling rind of safety
dripping hand over hand foot after foot body thrown onto dry deck exhausted
not to swim in that sweet water again.

January 27, 2007

Word User Jazz: Shut Down-n-Start

for poet, piano, base, Chinese broom on drum and iBook G4 (or upgrade)

Try this

Da da uh huh

make fists and stick out your index fingers

mumm da dumm du da ha ha hummmmmm

with some force straighten your arms index fingers pointing up and jab up into the air

pa paaaaaaa

then withdraw

wahaaaaaaaaaaaaaaaaaa

See

ummmm

tiny little black question marks falling from the left air hole....? ? ? ? ? ¿ ¿

Huuuu q s n'da i i i sssssssssssss

tiny little black exclamation marks falling from the right air hole ....! ! ! ! ! ¡ ¡ ¡

daa aaa aaa aaa o o o

confused Babel code of dots and pudgy vertical dashes

woah waaaaaah mo maaaaaaaaaaaa

Wrapped in keyboard blanket

shhhhhhhhhhh

sipping black coffee letters

Mmmm

again

tsk tsk

and again

tsk tsk tsk shhhhhhhhhh

snowy   spaces   fall

          haaaa   aaaaaaa   aaaaa

January/February

sh shhhh shhhhh d'laing a lang

control

Oooooooo

Apple

ahhhhhhhh

96

delete

pop

Ha!

whirrrrrrrrrrrrr whimmmmm

January 28, 2007

Children's Orchestra

health hiding in seed pod notes burst with irritation of bow, fingers or breath

ascending, descending flow of unseen hours release purity to air

resurrection of past passions awakened by children dressed in black

tone sign posts of days

feelings treble and base enter the children

flowing time and form cure each as a world and perhaps the world

emissaries of order

knees bent

hearts numinous

ancient tree formal

silver flutes of un-kissed eager breath

crescendo of parental hopes

January 28, 2007

$

warm water saturating dry soil
limp leaves slowly rising
aroma of relief
gratefulness perfume
do not assume
only one kind of green

February 26, 2007

Ahhhhhh!

both aware
dart acid glance
press squeeze in in
vent solve smooth out
sassafras laugh loud now
fermented wet sugar tongue
open fingers squeeze mm-tight
soft thigh mounds between each
beads of regret on upper lip milk tip
tight tumbling winter green speed
lowing purring weeping kissing
rosey rushing ester tangle full
and let go fleshy psalm in
cotton calm exhale

February 28, 2007

stars of david crystal peace

flizzies of tiny frozen dots in March morning passion dance
above juniper and brittle peach boughs and twigs
flurting white hovers and wisps
immune fall and swoop oblivious
unafraid of melting the life of their joy

March 2, 2007

Food of Fondness

Together sharing taste and texture
the gristle of camaraderie
rice vegan, barbeque beef, chocolate, Coke, pousse café.
How intimate can you be without sharing a meal?

March 3, 2007

separation

inness is from time to time

and time no real markers

those ticking clanging rulerd artifice of convenience and fear

the countless beloved names and will be named

its full flow in out off screen G-world

and all un-known existent other

so recognition: indigo bird on who's back Imagination flies

experience: the road that tatters shoes and hearts

knowledge: little synapses firing in valleys of brain

record its sssss like steam escaping

sssssssounds in the heavens

deadly snake warning

death rattle

thin membrane and laws separate everything

March 3, 2007

Greeley School, Winnetka

Two large faces looked down from above the blackboard:
Abraham Lincoln
who freed the slaves like God did for the Jews
and the large school clock
whose second hand taunted with the final five slow seconds
at the end of the day.

March 6, 2007

Time and the offscreen GWorld

seasons astounded: muddy, lush and flaming, knowledge in stone and icicle:
glow behind leaf, glassy winged insect clinging
seeing an iridescent Indigo Bunting once
glaciers gushing, gigantic storms building over engines of warmed seas
havoc, splendor, calm, extreme
natural metronomes of remembered times
moon slivers and swells

miracleTorah, eternityCross, Koran dominion, calm Buddah rejection, gods, drugs,
ecstasy
certainty of agreeing community transcendent core
rhythms rituals yearning

mass murder and mathematics stymie ancient names
they vanish like lemon pucker catalogued in off screen GWorld
  Are You there? Here? Did You draw this with words:
ululating women, marching troops, self-flagellation
Europe Jewless, Chernobyl birdless
deadly virus, Darfor hopeless
every detail deistically designed?

You're not really watching are You, my own ancient One,
off screen now in electric splendor or gOne.

when not in pain, grateful for breath, clapping hands,
full of Heschel's radical solution amazed
extra cup of wine on the table
laws followed good intent, waiting

crying while pealing reason's onion for logic's dinner
1s trip and end on their backs like a dash
0s roll, totter; and, fall

lifted kindly by imagination, prodigious effort, secret codes, unspoken languages in
suffering seasons

heart's schematic capture by knowledge vast web elegant
only healing scars affirm organic stymied Inness
synapses fire astonished in brain valleys
gnashing starry gassy heavens distant chaos myths and legends
music was will be
too much information: love slap, hate kiss
donkey talking seeing angel
death rattle
thin membrane broken
birthdeath usthem cleanunclean shaltshaltnot
.com currencyandcurrents
onWeflow

March 6, 2007

the secret life of sisters

six and four and a half

sisters crawling on hands and knees

on soft cool grass rectangle

walled by clipped privet hedge

hidden from all but each other

as one became a butterscotch stripped tabby

and the other

a pink nosed white angora

purring

smiling

sister play

March 27, 2007

Imaginary Friend/Real Friend

when passing the tropical motif curtains going up the narrow stairs

arguing with the one within

blaming the one within

confiding to the one

within

I spoke to my imaginary friend.

When passing the tropical motif curtains going up the narrow stairs

arguing with you

blaming you

confiding to you

my little sister

I spoke with my real friend.

March 27, 2007

Great Artist: Susan Jean Loewenherz

Your hands touched marble and it was never anonymous again
your sensual being transformed cold stone and made it represent you
warm, witty and wonderful.

March 28, 2007

The New Amsterdam

Eyes sky

eyes foam

eyes ocean

chin

eyes to each other

heads

rise

fall

heads in unison with the ship

ocean

sky

ocean

sisters understanding motion.

April 2007

Everywhere

Now joined to the secret global silent conversation
of the left behind
unique irreplaceable responses and laughs unheard
yearning in all languages
silence.

My fingers crave Susan dial 011390585776033 and lonely Paolo says my name in his
kind way
or 1-305-462-0071, now no answer, but hear the phrase "I can't get out from under,"
before Mom was really under
or WI-6-1573 to tell her that I am at Pammy's house and not to worry.

Revisiting places
looking for fathers in factories they worked twenty or thirty years
the first love streets of college towns
foggy Pacific fishing boat at dawn
the Lyric Opera House curtain rises.

Cashmere soft moments brush past Tower Road will you marry me beach
pink and white rustling taffeta dress with big sash Grama hand sewn for sweet sixteen
Opa's wine cellar bolted iron door, the green room of Tchaikovsky big dreams,
Ridgeway cherries, Hill Terrace flowering chestnut tree, thorny raspberry patch, tomato
bushes, basal, gooseberries, wild grape trellis three wrought iron cats, one smiling,
nestled in leaves.

Smells of Narina's Trattoria and the Old Red Star Inn
Lutz, Kuhn's, The Parthanon: saganaki flaming, German pancakes, Grama's rugalah,
Oma's oxtails, Dad's Oreo cookies with salami slices inserted.
Susan where are you!
Let's drink a margarita with a smokey mesquite floater tossed on top.

Aching loss unsolved

frayed one sided conversation

substance less embrace

no gifts to send

no hopes to defend.

Fendi, Chanel, Thai silk, Issey Miyake, Kenzo

Prada tan suade shoes, Balenciaga hang in closet quiet.

Beloved now ashes and bones while magnolia blossoms bloom in snow

the unborn never knowing you. We, united again, only in earth?

I can crawl in by mom; but, where will I find you, scattered everywhere?

Someone is seeing with your eyes.

You are resting with Colette in France.

Soon you will hide in Venice waiting for our return.

Unbothered by dark rain, you will be lulled by Julian growing up, voice changing,

laughing with your laugh in Seattle.

They will sneak you back to New York in pagan service

celebrate you: reefer music remember your dancing.

Afternoon smile on La Spezia shore

enjoying the humor penis tumbling out of the Mediterranean.

Someone will look down and reach for the smooth phallic marble stone

tumbled in warm sunlight sea

which once betrayed you but you survived.

April 6, 2007

Ballet

Mr Heinse is a short man with a hunch back.

He is playing piano accompaniment for the ballet class

at the Edna McRae School of Dance in the Fine Arts Building, Michigan Avenue, in Chicago.

Floor to ceiling mirrors reflect young girls and a few boys lined up at the barre practicing,

plié, battement tandu, échappé, grande battement, elèvé, changé, sixty eyes in the mirror.

The boys are wearing black leotards and tights. The girls are wearing pink or black tights and black leotards. If you touch their hair it is stiff, sprayed and twisted into a knot high on their heads.

There is one girl

can you see her?

she is twelve, she has a small pink Chinese gauze butterfly in her dark hair and her joy is getting crushed.

She is walking out onto the resin tossed wood floor. The dancers are divided in three groups. They dance an adagio. Identical. The studio is one hundred and one degrees, "good for muscles."

Chopin can barely breathe.

Miss Edna McRae is walking along the front of the dancers, black cane pounding with each of her steps. She is white haired. Her associate, Miss Davray who is younger is standing in the door judging, agreeing. Miss Davray is a dangerous enemy. If she doesn't like someone, Miss McRae won't like that person either.

Now Miss McRae is walking, cane pounding wood, near, between the mirror, and the dancers.

Her watery blue eyes notice the girl, and she thinks," Brat!"

"What are you doing!" She snarls, pulling the arm of the butterfly dancer around so fast that she is off balance. Miss McRae's face is very close to the girl's face. Her eyes so close that if she was love there might be a kiss; but, instead she says, her thin upper lip curled under, "Everybody in Chicago hates you!"

Mr Heinse stops playing. The girl meets her stare.
Now Miss McRae is holding the girl's arm so tightly that it is bleeding black and blue purple and brown under her leotard in the shapes of Miss McRae's fingers.

Miss McRae turns away and motions for the music to begin again. Schubert vibrates in the air from the will of Mr Heinse and his finger tips. The girls and boys practice grace and form.

At five o'clock, the butterfly dancer is sitting on the El train going home. She is crying quietly not noticing her self. A lady, a stranger, is watching her and cannot help herself, "What is wrong, dear?"
"Nothing."
"I have watched you cry on the El, last year and this year. What is wrong?"
"Nothing. I just had a ballet class."

At home the girl is quiet among the needs and demands of her brother and sisters and mother and father interrupted conversations phone ringing arguments radio snide remarks TV laughter. Who could write the family music of being ignored?
Her mother notices her. "What's wrong?"
"Miss McRae says that everybody in Chicago hates me."
"Everybody in Chicago doesn't know you."

April 11, 2007

Flint Poet

without future or past

no numbers

no colors

do not use understood words

try something else

forget senses

forget culture

and sex

now you are close

think of how to do it

you are the one

to see

and say

with

a spark.

April 22, 2007

Marble Sarcophagus

After years and years
of carving Carrara marble into penises, clay penii, penes in lavender Marano glass
and clitorises in marble, chlorides in bronze, clit clit clit in oils, clitori in play dough,
a snatch in oils
you had a vision
a new idea
and when you told me
your new passion to carve sarcophagi
artistic vision
to my recoil
stubborn adherence was your reaction.

Don't do it.
I've never presumed
to judge or suggest
or influence
your artistic being
but now I beg
don't do it.

Carving a container of death
may draw it near may
get the attention of emptiness.

Balenchine did a polio ballet for Tanaquil L'Clercq
and after she danced it she
wounded swan
polio afflicted
frozen dancer's body married to
genius choreographer
don't do it.

I begged with all debating power

in artist's bag

hours of sitting together

wine in hand

my not convincing

what artistic premonition

self expression cannot deny

but then unknowing

I thought it was artistic

expression

and didn't know

it was your life.

May 4, 2007

dust

there is dust in living
it is there
thin reminder on wood table
desk tops and appliances
floors
under beds
up high

and dust in dying
in the receding
thoughts
and phrases
photos
particular foods
in dread
in the earth

dust swirling
in sunlight slowly
in ritual dance
all the loved
the hated
the unknown
in thick column
calmly moving
sexuality of change.

May 4, 2007

UP

sheer mist
dots of rain
on window
motor running
passengers reading

jets waiting
to lift away
from Frankfort
for Tagel
lives
how can you be gone?

knowing you remains
words
your sculptures
the Buddah you
ah, with fractured third eye of pyrite

we will hold on to
standing outside of ourselves
laughing
outside of ourselves
passion road
inner music

Frankfort rain
You are present
here
lift off with the jet
or is it different there?
Are you lifted

always lifted now
beyond a roll and cheese
beyond shaking with life
always up now

"up with fun"

Frankfort-now-in-the-air

May 4, 2007

no carnival

Traffic in my hands
heart on the road
two glass balls and hollow erection
half full of
your dust
mission must
rest you carbon
soft stones gray
memory unquiet
this ride by vineyards day.

Venezia
white dashes
ribbons of white
nothing masks this.

la sorella
May 8, 2007

For Bob

your smile
a field of orange red
Tuscan poppies
a surprise
after a turn in the road

May 8, 2007
Parma, Italy

Venice is orange
neon orange pants
with two reflector stripes
red orange t shirts
yellow orange t shirts
brown orange trench coat
orange under
black back pack
orange shoes
orange pink sunset
on flowing tourists
caps orange
hot May sadness.

May 10, 2007

still

still still
light on top
mountain heavy
wordless

May 10, 2007
Bischofshofen, Austria

Bavaria on the Autobahn

a hawk on the
currents of phrases
waiting for an
idea to kill
amongst
grassy spring growth

May 14, 2007

remembering dayaynu kind of life

seams fraying

glue dry, tiles missing

phone ringing with the reminders of debt

children laughing

partner offers a glass of water

inspiration recorded

a good book

June 7, 2007

psalm of permission

Veins of complex connections
black ink
lifeblood of words gone liquid
flowing wet the trail glistens and then dries.

Bellows to my heart
chance after chance to embrace tactile knowing unmasked
not understanding what to do
when the time comes
not given permission
only dusted with commandments.

What did I do
did I say something while she screamed in pain?
Did I run into the room and shout,
Mercy! pushing away scrubs thoughtless engine speeding procedure?
No.
I stood in the hall and wept empty hands while they were hurting my mother.

Every instant artesian chance to rise up
curling sweet pea shoot music seeking flush
petals radiant iridescent fuchsia.

Contracted holiness
left us alone
clutching small distractions
stumbling drunken
offering borrowed thoughts
unaware
lying.

Repository of hope

check, code, scan the heart flinging unknown into distant intuitive fear
splendor unexpected rests and patterns await
silver cup forgotten fulfillment holy this is you
ecstasy of kindness, courage, core
be
do

June 10, 2007

the younger dryas

sudden long lasting freeze
susan sudden leaving breath
earthy hot younger sister dressed in dewy web silk hemp smoke and oak
twelve hundred years may pass then be done unfold you laughing
but in the music of trees you gather strength and warm and warm me now

June 11, 2007

colored ropes of silk around an ancient tree

no matter what else is happening, in the morning there
the barges are slowly pulled
on the Chao Phraya
and in the Shangra La
barefoot maids with sweet smiles smooth fresh sheets

June 11, 2007

Susan for President

Pagan reveler
anarchist
freedom fighter for sensuality
rub it in your face art
expatriate identity
intuitive grace:

Susan for President!

Every year you ran for president and
printed a different campaign slogan
on cards.

Up with Fun in '91

Being Free in '93

Loving More in '94

Sometimes the cards had little drawings of erect penises saluting
the motto of their commander and chief:

Susan for President!

This year the slogan on the cards you made but didn't distribute:

I'm in Heaven in 2007.

How could you! so droll
diabetes, cancer, chemo
nonchalant response
to hopes of you swimming back to health to us

letting us know
oscarwildesque
amused at leaving
done with life
tossing it like a card
ta ta blithe over it.

You didn't want to be president.
You didn't believe in heaven.

June 28, 2007

7787

July haiku of questions
lavender recognition
a motor starting in the dark
at 3:43 A.M.

July 21, 2007

Grace

I'm trying not to forget the feeling of grace.

The old man was afraid when he received the oracle.
He whispered," It can be lost."

Broken stalk
   weeping
      confused schemes
         very busy duties
            quest un-aware
               muffled Pan Pipes turned head instant
available.

Flushed pink hot neck
   beads of water syncopate down shoulders and thighs
      naked in summer phlox
         night air
           taste of fresh figs
sixteen

eighty-six

it's all the same with this thrilling breath.

July 26, 2007

creamy white water lily singing the moisture of its yellow center

aroma of humid heat in sunlight

petals serene evening close

torn asunder by black night unseen predator teeth

open bloom and torn at once

spin

teeth and bloom

all

shuttleing forward and back

time cracked time veneer time

small pulse disappearing into

hhhhhhhhhhhh

July 28, 2007

Planning

Whiplash chartreuse change
a shock
expectations harbored rouge!

Pushing forward
wrong as a comma
in a w,ord
actions absurd
clear sticky fluid wrung out of hope.

Jagged broken edge
fine lines askew
hoax timesavers ridicule control.

Door stuck
cuts stun design
glut of electronic and wooden woe
scheduled to know.

August 11, 2007

Things are crazy here: lots of people, crying baby, dishwasher broken, roof leaking, bath tub not draining, people's sleepless emotionals, smoke detector loudly sawing the air as the toast burns.

August 18, 2007

no frolic and running

Since you died I've reached for navy blue
small patterns
rigorous finishing
clean and spare.

August 19, 2007

while they sleep

rumbling night rolling thunder
glassy dark august rain
roof and walk tonal water breath
ten thousand feet distance running
black sky full of military jets
zinnias orange-red dancing yellow stars round erect nipple bristling center unseeing eyes
dusty blonde pistils bulging stamens erect pollen tubes
petals neon purple sepals chartreuse
full vases in dark rooms
refrigerated green jacketed bicolor corn
hairloom tomatoes
smoked cheese sweet peaches lacey cauliflower
closeted clothes pressed together
cotton covered sleeping beloved bodies
wedding dreams wandering
dark night
white sound

August 19, 2007

Poets' September Tour of Chicago and Vicinity

Each afternoon at least eighteen poets drive south on Lake Shore Drive
and watch the Hancock Building lower slowly as they dictate into their pocket
recorders. At the Museum of Contemporary Art, poets contemplate a bowl of commas
    by crossover poet artist Don,tyouwish.
Taylor Street cop poets eat hearty portions of pizza at *Pompei* and rank on each other
with arresting poems of pushers and family disputes.
Purple line passengers don't notice the moleskin or the hooded rider
    writing sexual back porch poems to the screech and clack.
Children's sidewalk chalk poems on Bissell and Cleveland, stretch long and wash away
with the rain.
In the Garfield Park jungle, coco pods hang from the trees,
    rap poetry roots of deeds.
On Western and Devon the ragged Pigeon Man feeds a hundred birds and sees poetry
in their wings, pecks and swoops as passers by are revolted.
The crack of a bat, a boy is hot dog happy hearing the ball game poetry
    that his father sings so proudly.
O'Hare and Midway planes ascend and descend, silvery phrases of sitting souls.
At the Lalique store on Michigan Avenue, a lady surrounds her finger with beautiful
sand that imperceptibly moves but seems solid
    the color of a pool's deep end.
A poem is written with a stick in the sand at Bryn Mawr beach and eaten by a wave of
the hungry lake.
The Brother's K, little tables and a collection of Friday night poets,
    caffeine and words' nervous energy.
Mexican pastry in Pilsen, one syllable taste bud elongated exclamations.
At the Green Mill, martini men and women mangle tenderness so beautifully.
Some diamonds shine blue in the Café black light where poems are sometimes mistaken
for friendship.
Rosehill, Memorial Park, and Waldheim spawn poetry of broken branches.
Kabuki master dances both male and female roles in costumed splendor.
Melvin Taylor plays blues poetry with fingers running like a spider on crack up the neck
of his guitar; and, at the top, wrist turned fingers running down the neck in a hurry.

Emanuel cantor Shelly Drucker-Friedman sings the poetry of atonement to a congregation slowing in their yearly reasons to atone. Their rubber tip cane pleas transform and transfer to benefit others.

Cardinal George: the meaning of red knowing the nativity of awe.

Bees buzz on top of City Hall and their honey is collected daily malaprop free with finesse by the late Richard J.'s mayor son Richard M., poet of the green city that works. The Lincoln Park Zoo rhino has a thinking, critical, lyrical evolution of its lumbering prehistoric past

visiting the Evanston Public library at 1:30 P.M. on the fourth Friday of each month.

September 4, 2007

141

Painful Privilege

When he was born she was second.
His hungry sucking mouth
her mother's attention consumed.
Her father wanted a son and got him;
his voice rises when he acknowledges his son and falls in the same breath when he adds
recognition of his daughter.

Now twelve,
her private school gives her three hours of homework a night.
She has other lessons after school.
She was seen pulling out her hair.
They gave her Ritalin to make it better.

Her brother taunts her.
She hits him.
She is punished for hitting him.
Hating herself for losing control she always hits him when he does it.
Angry father, mother, brother, at her.

No one has told her
hitting him makes her miserable.
She has tools:
she could shun his provocative taunts
or react with dismissive laughing
or just let him know,
"I'm over it."

What would she be like if her mother
stopped the pills and took her out of school?
They could have breakfast in their pajamas, get dressed and take a walk.
She would not need to compete.
Mother and daughter could talk about the world.

She and her mother could write a book together and illustrate it,

relax,

read, do math problems and go out to lunch.

Home school.

Laugh.

Take a train ride.

Go to museums.

Enjoy quiet.

Enjoy music, many different kinds.

Her brother would be at school.

She would be with her mother alone.

Loved and considered,

not a child left behind her own spirit of mystery and joy.

September 6, 2007

neurosis friendalota

exotic neurotic tic & twitch

electric fast attention switch

to fried food or pollen fear, grilled salmon, grandchildren

anger knob made of dough to burn

pride swelling kvelling open the door to sameness uneasy yearn

cunning conversation fragments

eyes darting after hearing

around the room

September 27, 2007

Mapping In Contiguous Spaces and Incompatible Times

Where is the jar of manna stored
  of taste craved
  and satisfaction assured?

Surveying packed earth with dusty boots
  collecting data and chewing power bars
  far remote sensing on atmospheric curve
  maps the terrain of we who've lost our nerve.

With our enhanced special resolution
  pixel details perfect
  we see looting in progress
  with no court of redress.

Snaky rivers, gates and ancient roads
  crazy-quilt of grassy shades and hilly shapes
  no understanding of the mountain water fresh words
  of the living
  surmise and speculation
  about the dead.

Footprint location
  policy application
  where Moses is buried
  if the place can be found
  best never.

Oogle earth and see what can no longer be seen
  in increments of three hundred and sixty years or a thousand
  over-burdened with meters, matters and degrees
  sending electrical pulse into the soil
  vaccinating its secrets.

Walking through data sets
   we can tell exactly who we are
   where we are
   what we want to do.

We want to do it to them
   they to want to do it to us
   children of the dead soon to be dead
   holding promises to our chests
   statistics of action.

Modeling the heat
   there was burning, red
   there was very heavy burning, redder
   huge amounts of burning, black.

There seems to be nothing there now
   archeologists simulating virtual people
   walking reconstructed vanished streets
   shoveling away overburden
   drawing conclusions from
   fragment inscriptions.

Inferences and dry artifacts
   expectations revisited time
   our decline.

September 29, 2007

Plum Tree

We should have known
when after the storm
the trunk of the plum tree snapped
and its crown
laden with fruit
leaned against our home
like a head on a shoulder
and then you arrived
frail and sweet.

We picked the fruit off the branches
and saved it.
But we couldn't save you.

October 1, 2007

where are you
sister friend
empty my un-made phone calls
this end frayed flapping in fall wind
unsightly dark circles and hesitance
sleepless single malt desperation
knowing all the while your desire to celebrate
clinched brain my pink glass fractured splinters of
wanting you alive

October 2, 2007

Earth bound

I live on a distant spiral

arm

not in the center

but

this moment

you

are the

center

for me

I, the very un-centered

and you, the absent.

October 2, 2007

Navigating the Big Lake

Seven miles out
you begin to disappear.

Race tracking
twenty foot waves
rogue wave lifts tons air-born.

A map always starts with a request.
I am floundering.
"Find her."

October 2, 2007

the living half of the hourglass

. words written to the dead

. un-established efficacy

. un-believed power

. silent yearning

. forgiveness

. asking

. being

. lost

. on

. land

. living

. without

. still present

. memory and love

. sounds of screams

. silenced for years still audible

October 3, 2007

crazy is catching

amazing how a bum rap sticks

parcour of principles

some occasions risk slips

October 5, 2007

Forcing me treadmill to do deep breaths what I good health want by
your gym shoe guidance gentle urging the stay strong live long for me
when I vegetables in vodka overeating sleepless do
so I won't rue.

October 6, 2007

there is so much joy in loss
joy eaten voraciously by absence
what is this swimming solace
the Hollywood thirty's musicals of
tapping smiles and glamour
life entertaining itself grandly
in the style of heaven
Thai dinners and lavish tea
long car trip on route 66
dear sister and me
life and death now mixed

October 7, 2007

Downburst

Ominous dense dark shelf cloud angry weight too heavy darker unexpected wind black
cloud lowers and lowers pointing damp wet finger at earth with straight-line winds too
heavy for thundering air.
Suddenly seek shelter
violence warm and cool collide
gusts and limbs snapping
homes splintering
lives lost in mythic frame of natural chaotic eighty mile an hour no blame
as the finger of the storm dissipates pulled into the thundering updraft of the traveling
event on its way East.

October 20, 2007

Pegasus and the Laugh

both of us
sad and dwelling on loss
faced each other
at a loss

you praised me
admired me
guided me to
think happier
the same guidance I had
for you

the next day
you uncomfortable too overwhelmed to go
I went

the study group gathered
I wrote a laugh in a small notebook
in attempt to leap from your fears and pain
mixed with my sadness

When You Laugh

twinkling flavors
salt and sweet
annotated aromas
note and tone moan woody and floral
solo and choral color complex
paint chart passionate series of reds
pinks, corals, egg yolk yellow
pumpkin seeds and strings in squishy weave complex

            honey of resolution paradox smoothed
                bouncing breath exhaled moist
                    pattern pods burst
                       your laughter

and when asked to turn in the Sonchino St. James version to Genesis 18:15 on page 88
I realized it was Sarah's laugh I wrote
the rest of the morning was commentary:
Kittel, Aquila, versio arabia, versio aethopica, versio armenica

after lunch you searched in boxes with our diplomat son in law
my cousin's daughter applying to medical school
her friend the Latin teacher
went on their way

I was left with John Ashbury, Louise Gluck, Anthony Hecht and W. S. Merwin
each reading their poems to me and speaking of writing
Hecht's 'incontinent sadness' and Merwin's tropical garden stayed

the second margarita tilted us to choose Midwestern kindness over spectacular blues
after David Lynch video cornfields and brotherly yearning reparation journey
we slept

I awoke to a nikker
Pegasus made of moving gold dust nuzzled my arm
I was smaller than a mother of pearl blouse button
you could roll over and crush me so I climbed up a thread count cotton fold onto
Pegasus between his neck and wings
and we flew
through the closet door
silk robe and hemp jacket
smooth and scratchey canyon
through the wall and out above Ridge Avenue

sparse cars

past the arching elms

in darkness we flew

harvest moon below us

until he settled into his constellation

me now gigantic example of the Rose Center for earth and space

if I could write Sarah's annunciation laugh before I read it happened

long after it happened

O'Keefe's clouds now minute

from this starry perch

perhaps joy is still available for me for you

October 28, 2007

reading the leaves

that certain freezing night rain when the yellow leaves fall
permission wet tight knots untied

blue eyes angled glance to the side submission
wide want closing tight like a lens

contrition uncut melon orange soft center seeds
hidden in dark enclosed in rivulet ridged rind

out of the gate ambition cacophonous applause smiles special favors
red and black satin giddy whipping runs miles miles miles old bones

elbowing mission through crowds and shrouds
lavender perfume of justice stone steps high into electric mist

behind back choosing moving pawns with unique faces on board heaving digital see
laughing stronger opponent smoke curls up

flaunting what will be lost
soon forgotten words and rings

repetition of haunting sensory reminders: Tuesday siren, dental drill, white pearls falling
on gray marble, reaching under the bed finding dust, new chores

dawn wishing cup of hot green tea night leaves
no telling strip of paper wisdom
rosy cirrus cloud

November 15, 2007

159

Electronic Talking Bird

He bought an electronic talking bird and talks to it.
"I love you, I love you, I love you,"
and the bird repeats that.

She said he is behaving like a little boy.
She told me to listen,
"I love you," she said.
The electronic bird said,
"I love you."

Perhaps they do not say those words to each other anymore
or they like a guaranteed response
or the meaning is dulled
or novelty is all that is left
but who can guess
at deep bonds of marriage?

November 20, 2007

emerald healing stone

warm clear morning sunlight entering into emerald healing stone
if I had written those words then
and you had read them
and known
then eaten the paper they rested on
overthrown deadly cells could have stopped
and you would have grown old
useless words

November 21, 2007

breath

sitting so still

palms up

calm breath

new power to play musical instruments, bandoneon, bandore, banjo

they form and become weighty in my hands

realization of languages unspoken, untaught, becoming poems between my breaths

images of Bangladesh cyclone sufferers spared death grouped by muddy banks

wrapped in warm blankets, given hot food and hope

and then breath

and breath and

breath

November 21, 2007

Ocean Sheridan Hart Timmins

Born 11/24/06

The week before you came
on the other side of the country
your cousin repeated your name
the name we did not know,
"Ocean", "Ocean", "Ocean",
again and again all week
with infant baby knowing
like one of Midnight's Children
calling your name, announcing your coming
a herald of joy.
Your uncle said, "He will have oceans of love."
I held you, Oona's newborn boy,
our newborn soul of great joy
my failures blew away like dry leaves.

December 1, 2006

tesserae of thought

loose piles grouped by color

carefully laid in patterns and forms

ancient remnants and of this moment

glazed clay, glass, marble, mother of pearl

wood, edge of cloud, light and dark

mis/broken

understood

evil

good

December 3, 2007

a la Duduki

Yesterday was the anniversary of my late mother's birth

yesterday our daughter told us that she is pregnant

we visited mother's grave

and bought food for a party

I went to a Chicago Symphony Orchestra concert

Rachmaninov No. 4 in G Minor, Op. 40

Janacek

but something else

something astonishing

new

Mark Elder, the conductor

played a recording of Duduki music, music from Georgia

with droning accompaniment

then

the orchestra began the Kancheli composition inspired by that haunting instrument

the tonal alchemy transformed memories into presence

from immediate sadness rose a joy that filled the hall

and I recognized it

the presence of my mother

that music was so powerful it could bring the dead to life

and it did.

December 14, 2007

Mary Wells

old music aged wine of vibration my situation unselfconscious abandon to sequence
voice and sax
relax
this time isn't that
but it rhymes

December 26, 2007

Chung King Mansions

Hot humid night hearts beating
neon Hong Kong July late street crowds
Beggar's Chicken golden mallet breaking crust with Mother's ginger pound
lettuce wrapped pigeon, deep fried lamb, lemon fish, black mushrooms, pea pods.

Back alone awake in dark silent room
I stared out the window at the Chung King Mansions
light green glow in one room, dark stain on the outside of the building like a falling man
no motion in forty windows where stickings were common in urine odor halls.

Up on the hot roof
silhouette of a man standing in the Kowloon heat.
I watched unseen.
He motionless for a long time haloed by neon saturated black sky
slowly raised his hand to his mouth
hot orange pin point glow inhale
his arm lowered
he stood still then slipped out of sight.

January 2, 2008

www.ingramcontent.com/pod-product-compliance
Lightning Source LLC
LaVergne TN
LVHW011233080426
835509LV00005B/485